LIFE LESSONS ON ICE

LIFE LESSONS ON ICE

J.K. Tinkham

Writers Club Press
San Jose New York Lincoln Shanghai

Life Lessons On Ice

Writers Club Press
an imprint of iUniverse, Inc.

For information address:
iUniverse, Inc.
5220 S. 16th St., Suite 200
Lincoln, NE 68512
www.iuniverse.com

Not only for young hockey players but also for their parents and coaches.

ISBN: 0-595-21685-4

Printed in the United States of America

This book is dedicated to all the young and not so young

hockey players who play the game because they love it

for everything that it was, is and will be in their lives.

Early Morning Ice

By J.K. Tinkham

The alarm is set for 4am
That's what time he has to wake up in order to make it to practice.
4am! Everyone else in the world is asleep.
Everyone: except for the rest of his team.

Why do we have to practice this early again?
Somewhere in his mind he is thinking those very thoughts.
Who scheduled this practice anyway?
Half the team will probably oversleep.

He stumbles out of bed
Looks at the shower and decides, why bother.
He brushes his teeth, splashes water on his face,
throws on his warm ups and is out the door.

On his way to the rink he is thinking how stupid
he was for leaving his bag in the car the night before.
Now he is going to have to put on damp, frozen skates.
That should wake him up.

Okay, he says to himself, get your mind right.
A lot of skating today.
We need to work hard.
What was it we were supposed to practice today anyway?

He finishes lacing up his skates, grabs his stick and glides out onto the ice.
Hard smooth ice. It's like glass.
There's nothing better.
Looking around he realizes that the rest of his team did show up.
Looks like this is going to be a good practice after all.
He's awake now. Time to start.

He makes a couple of fast turns around the rink
Enough to warm up and shake off the chill.
He looks around at the rest of his team on the ice,
Nods his head at a couple of guys standing beside him,
Blows his whistle and starts practice.

WHAT A HOCKEY PARENT SAYS ABOUT "LIFE LESSONS ON ICE"

"Life Lessons On Ice" is a poignant look at the parallels, paradoxes and pitfalls that a young player faces not only in hockey but also, and more importantly, in life. It is a thought-provoking and engaging book that speaks to the trials and tribulations that every player must deal with. It encourages these young men and women to be prepared for life, take responsibility for their own happiness, implement a plan or blueprint for their future, remain flexible and be willing to adapt and take time to reflect as they confront the many challenges that lie ahead.

For me, this was a compelling account of the issues I struggled with as a youth and contend with as an adult at and away from the hockey rink. The analogies and illustrations were sharp and insightful. The reader finds themselves soul-searching and contemplating the question, "What is my life's mission?"

This book truly captures the heart of the player, coach, parent and fan. I know because I have been all of these at one time or another. It helps equip the player to meet the many challenges and obstacles that hockey and life will surely present. "Life Lessons on Ice" provides a refreshing perspective and helps instill a sense of pride, purpose and passion to the player's game on and off the ice!

Bob Bonisolli, Hockey Parent*

(author's note: *and Travel Hockey Team Manager Extraordinaire)

"Life Lessons On Ice"
FOREWORD
by Ken Hitchcock
1999 Stanley Cup Winning Coach
2002 Olympic Gold Medal Winning
Assistant Coach/Canada

When I first read Kim's manuscript, it brought back many great memories of playing sports on all my teams back in Canada. At that time I didn't know why I liked to play on teams so much, but it was later in life that I discovered the answer. Upon understanding the impact that team sports had on my life, I really felt that if someone could ever express that information to children and parents, it would help people understand the importance of playing in that type of community.

Kim has created a clear and concise perspective of the role of sports, Ice Hockey in particular, and the effects they have on our lives. Playing on a team promotes not only personal growth but can shape you into a valued member of society. The lessons I learned are just now beginning to take hold in me, and hopefully experiencing this book can invoke the understanding of how playing Ice Hockey parallels so many other aspects of our lives. I'm sure you will find this book extremely educational. Happy learning!

Yours in Hockey,

Ken Hitchcock

"Thank You" to the following people who played a
significant part in this book being written

My wonderful parents, Carl and Yukiko Ponder,
for setting my feet on the right path.

Two special people, Don and Carole Tinkham,
for showing a continued interest in everything that I do.

Stacey Oleksa,
for her friendship and encouragement.

And a special thank you to my husband, Scott,
for sharing his stories and his love of the game with me.

INTRODUCTION TO 'LIFE LESSONS ON ICE'

Why I wrote this book ...

Not long ago I witnessed what I felt was the worst display of parental "cry babying" I have ever seen in my years in ice hockey and youth sports in general. It was supposed to be a friendly game. It turned out to be a lesson that the few involved would find hard to forget. It wasn't what happened on the ice that made it so terrible. It was what happened off the ice after the game.

The teams on paper were definitely not evenly matched. The underdog team was the Bantam House team. For those of you who aren't familiar with youth ice hockey a Bantam House team usually consists of 13 and 14 year olds. Some of these players are good. Most are mediocre at best. All of them are there to play hockey and have fun. The team highly favored to win the scrimmage was a Pee-Wee Travel Team. A Pee-Wee Travel team usually consists of 11-12 year olds that are seasoned skaters and good stick handlers. Competitive hockey.

Coaches of both teams had agreed to play each other. The coach of the Bantam team thought it would be a good introduction to his players to see what Travel hockey was all about. The coach of the Pee-Wee Travel team thought it would be a good warm-up for an upcoming weekend tournament.

At the drop of the puck everything changed. The Bantam team, having nothing to lose and everything to gain, played position, passed the puck and in general just played really consistent hockey. The Pee-Wee team, over-confident and undisciplined on this particular day, fell apart after the first period losing six to two at the final buzzer.

I have to tell you that it was an exciting game. The players seemed to have fun even though the coach of the Pee-Wee team was getting angrier as the gap in the score widened. I believe that he, like any good coach, was disappointed that his players were not taking the game seriously. There was a fair amount of checking. The officials called what they saw and penalties were doled out evenly. The one big difference in the game was that only one team really showed up to play. By the middle of the third period it was evident which team had shown up.

The players skated to center ice to do the obligatory handshake and sportsmanship "good game" mumble. That was it. They all went to their respective dressing rooms and it was over.

Not quite, in the lobby of the ice rink overlooking the sheet of ice that had just hosted the game the Zamboni began doing its job and some of the parents of the Travel Team started making their excuses.

It was decided among the loudest of the group that the reason that their team had lost was because there had been a "ringer" placed on the Bantam team. That's right, a ringer. The "ringer" was another Bantam that actually played on a Bantam Travel team. He was tall. He was fast. He was dominant on the ice. He was thirteen. He wanted to win. *That's the reason they lost.* The other team just couldn't stop this guy. He was too much. He was dominant *even* when his line wasn't on the ice. He was the reason they had lost. Never mind that the travel team deserved to lose because they didn't want it bad enough. They didn't show up for the game. But, that was okay because these parents gave them all an excuse. Let's blame it on someone else. Let's blame it on this other kid and the coach that let him play!

As the excuses multiplied I found myself getting angry, then frustrated and then back to angry. I couldn't understand what was going on. Why was this affecting me so? Why did it matter to me what these parents were doing? This same scenario had been acted out in every youth sport my son had chosen to participate in whenever parents forgot that the game was for the kids. Then the reason occurred to me. This was different. I really loved the game of hockey. I loved watching these kids play. I loved the lessons that they were learning as they played this great game. I loved... I snapped... "Hey! You wouldn't be making these excuses if you had won"! There, I said it. It was over. Not really, but for the sake of this story let's call it over. The repercussions would haunt me for a couple of days but I would come through it none the worse for wear.

What made me snap? I loved the game. I had come to realize in the past few years watching my son play that this was a great preview to life; this Great Game on ice. Until a decade ago I had not even seen hockey played on television much less in person. I fell in love with the game the moment I saw it. It was fast. It was aggressive. It was graceful. It was great fun to watch!

I had come to realize that within the game of hockey were hidden "Life Lessons". Lessons that my son would find during the hours of practice and games and tryouts and in the dressing rooms. I wanted him to find these lessons and to understand them. That's what this book is all about. As a parent, I'm old enough to realize the lessons ahead of time for him. I'm writing this book for my son and all the other young hockey players so that they can find those lessons early and with as little "experiential pain" as possible.

And just like in the game of hockey, life is not all about winning, it's about "keeping your head up and your stick on the ice"!

A special note to parents. Youth Hockey, as is any youth sport, is a great way to teach your kids about life and the lessons they will encounter. Take the opportunity to use the game as a teaching tool. Show your kids what good sportsmanship is all about; don't just talk about it. Don't make excuses or place blame on someone else because of a loss. Don't put pressure on your kids to do something that if the truth were known you yourself would find hard to do. Talk to them about how important good character is on and off the ice. And most importantly, just like in real life, tell them that things will not always go the way they planned. Sometimes, you learn more from losing than from winning. A great thing to remember is that even when a sport isn't used to build character, it will definitely reveal it.

CONTENTS

The male pronoun "he" has been used throughout the book for the sake of convenience. I do recognize that the game of hockey is played and coached by women as well as men and it is my hope that all youth hockey players, their parents and coaches will enjoy this book.

God grant me the serenity to accept the things I cannot change, the courage to change the things I can, and the wisdom to know the difference.

~ Reinhold Niebuhr ~

CHAPTER ONE

THE ICE WILL NOT ALWAYS BE PERFECT

As a hockey player you'll hear it a thousand times. "Man, that ice was perfect" or "Geez, this ice is slow". Life is like that. You'll have your good days and your bad days. Some of you may even have your bad years. But life is like playing hockey. Whether or not you decide to skate, the ice will remain the same and (unless you are God or at least the Zamboni driver) you won't change it. The only thing that you can do is to decide whether or not to skate and whether or not you will make the best of the situation.

Your life will have the same ruts in it like ice that has played host to a hundred figure skaters. It won't be smooth all of the time. After all, the Zamboni can only do so much. Think about it. Hockey players that are eager to get out on the ice and are concentrating more on the game, the big picture, won't find themselves complaining about it as much. They just want the ice time. Life can be like that. Be excited about it! Look forward to the feel of skating on it. All the complaining in the world won't change the condition of the ice. Jump out there and take control of what you can take control of...YOU.

Remember, no matter how good you are as a skater there will be times when you fall. Sometimes, you'll fall because someone checked you into the boards and really cleaned your clock. Sometimes you will fall because you got hooked. Sometimes you will fall because you just hit a bad spot on the ice. Whatever the reason and no matter how you look when you fall down there is a very good chance that you will be able to get back onto your feet and continue the game. Life is like that. You will fall down. Maybe not physically; but mentally and emotionally. You can't always be "up".

Falling down in life might mean failing a test that you really needed to ace to pass the class. You may have really studied but the answers just didn't come to you during the test. Your mind just went blank. You fell down. Get back up. It may be the end of the game but it's not the end of your life.

Maybe your girlfriend just told you that she doesn't want to be your girlfriend anymore. You stand there by your locker feeling your feet start sliding out from beneath your body. Talk about receiving a cheap shot without the ref seeing it! You feel like you are taking a head first dive into the boards. Hey, keep your head up! Assuming you don't go crashing through the boards you'll get back up. It may be the end of the game but it's not the end of your life.

You may hear one of your friends telling other people about how badly you played last weekend. Everyone is laughing. You just had a bad game. You feel miserable. You want to hide in a locker. Better yet, you want to slam him into a locker. Right now you can't feel anything other than how mad you are at him for making fun of you and at yourself for playing so poorly. It's like skating over rough ice. It feels terrible. You can hardly do anything on it and the whole time you are skating on it all you can think of is how bad it is. Keep skating. If you fall, get up. You can lie there if you want but all you will get out of it is cold. There is no uglier sight than a hockey player imitating a puck. No one will even remember you "falling" unless you make a big deal out of it.

An ancient saying goes "you can never cross the same river twice." Makes sense to me. The water is constantly moving. The next time you cross the river it's over different water.

Life is like that. So is hockey. You get another chance to skate on a fresh sheet of ice after every period or at least every game. The Zamboni comes through and does its job and you find yourself skating on a new sheet of ice. Things change.

When you find yourself sitting on the bench of your life, waiting to get on and you realize that the ice isn't perfect, don't wait. You may find yourself like a lot of people that are older than you spending your whole life waiting for the perfect 'sheet of ice' or circumstance or opportunity or situation. Just skate out on the ice and do what you are there to do. Play hockey. Enjoy your life now before it melts away!

Off Ice Training Exercise

Write five things that you would do if you had the perfect life.
What's stopping you from doing those things now?

When you're prepared, you're more confident.
When you have a strategy, you're more comfortable.
~ Fred Couples ~

Chapter Two

In the Game of Life, Just As In Hockey, You Have To Be Prepared

I know quite a few hockey players that have a recurring nightmare. They dream that they get to the rink before an important game and they have forgotten their skates or their stick or their helmet. There is not enough time to go back to get the missing equipment so they sit on the bench while everyone else plays. What a terrible nightmare!

Well, do you know how many of you have done that very thing? Be honest. You forgot, and either your Mom or Dad or little sister reminded you that you left your helmet or other necessary piece of equipment. Of course, they did remind you before you left the driveway. That was close! Life won't be so accommodating.

You have to be prepared. You have to think ahead. Something that a lot of kids aren't great at doing. They really should teach a class in school called "Being Prepared 101". How many of you have actually said things like, "I remembered it after it was too late", or "I was going to do it but I forgot", or the granddaddy of them all "you should have reminded me"! You do know that NHL players don't have their Moms following along on their trips making sure that their bags are packed. You do know that right?

Enough about the obvious. How do we change all of that? Tools. You have to use tools. I'm not talking about hammers and screwdrivers, unless of course, you'd like to use a stapler to staple the reminder note on your forehead. By using tools, I mean making lists and keeping them attached to things that you know you won't forget. One hockey player I know made a nice neat list of all his equipment. He laminated it and attached it to his hockey bag. Before every game he goes and looks over the list and makes sure that he has everything.

Calendars are great tools. Go get your favorite type of calendar and start writing down your schedule on it. That way you won't have to keep apologizing for forgetting that you were supposed to be somewhere or do something. Remember, it's your responsibility to know when your practices and games are scheduled. You might even find it helpful to write down which teams you are playing in a game so you can be mentally prepared. Hang the calendar up in a place that you have to see it every morning. In the bathroom next to the mirror is a good place.

Hockey tape. Yep, that old standby. I could have been rich by now just selling hockey tape to players that didn't come prepared. And you know the old story. It's an early morning game and the pro shop isn't open yet and you have no tape to re-tape your stick or any to tape your socks. And neither does anyone else! Be prepared. It will not only save you from embarrassing moments but will start you on a good habit for life. I have always loved the Boy Scout motto "be prepared".

As you get older you will find that your usual tool for reminding you what is going on (let's call her Mom) isn't around. Maybe you are at a hockey camp in Canada or in college. Maybe you have graduated and have started a new job as Assistant Marketing Director for ESPN. Congratulations! You can't afford to forget something. You can't blow things off and not be ready for a meeting. You have to have done your homework in advance or you won't have to worry about your job. You just won't have one. Talk about a preparedness nightmare.

As you get older you will have little things that will show you that you are not prepared enough. Like when you start to drive. If you run out of gas, the car is telling you something. If you are asked last minute to escort the most popular girl in school to a dinner where she is getting an award (her boyfriend has come down with the flu) and your one good suit is sitting at the bottom of your closet in a crumpled mess. That's telling you something.

Here is a scenario. After a hockey game in which your team has beaten the National Champions, a television reporter walks up to you; sticks a microphone in your face and says "tell our viewers how your team was able to beat last year's champions". There you are. How prepared are you now? Whatever you do don't say something stupid and for heaven's sake don't use profanity! What will you do? You have to be prepared for moments like this. Have you ever noticed that intelligent athletes all sound the same when they are interviewed? They say things like, 'we just played position, played as a team and never gave up'.

They practice on those answers just in case. They are prepared.

It is not enough in life or in hockey to "think" you are prepared. You have to "know" you are prepared.

Off Ice Training Exercise

Your team has just won the Division I NCAA Championship.
A reporter from Hockey News asks you,
"How does it feel and to what do you attribute the
success of your team?"

What are you going to say?

Some self-confronting questions: "Where do I want to be at any given time?" "How am I going to get there? "What do I have to do to get myself from where I am to where I want to be?"... "What's the first, small step I can take to get moving?"
~ George A Ford ~

CHAPTER THREE

YOU HAVE TO HAVE A PLAN

Have you ever seen a hockey team with a coach that didn't have a plan on how to play the other team? Definitely not a pretty sight. How about if each player skated until he was good and ready to come off the ice and then slowly skated off the ice? Have you ever given much thought to what the NHL has to go through to plan out the different games between different teams during the hockey season? What if they just said, "Hey, play when you want and play who you want." What if each rink you played at had different rules for the game. It would be mass chaos.

Well, you know…you guessed it…that's what life is like. You have to have a plan in order to know what you need to do. Life doesn't just happen. At least not the way you want it to if you don't have a plan. How do you make a plan for your life?

First, you have to have some goals. What is a goal? Goal: an object of a person's ambition or effort; destination or aim. Most NHL hockey teams' goal is to win Lord Stanley's Cup. In youth hockey your goal might be to win the play-offs. Just like your team must have goals, you must have goals. What are your goals in life? Start thinking about what you want your goals in life to be. What is it that you want to accomplish?

Need some help with this? There are a ton of books out there that will show you how to put down in writing your goals and the action steps that will help you to achieve them. One of my all time favorites (I liked it so much I began teaching it) is called "The Path" by Laurie Beth Jones. Great how-to book. Easy to read and will walk you through the different steps. It will take you a step further in your self-learning process and help you to find out what your mission in life might be. Everyone is born with a purpose. You are no different.

Take your time with this because it is important. It's so important that I'll take questions via e-mail about how you can do this. You'll find my e-mail address at the end of this book.

After you figure out what some of your goals in life might be, then your next step is to develop a plan of action. Don't worry, people's goals change a little as they get older. Unless they totally give up on a goal (which means it wasn't really their goal after all) they end up fine tuning it.

A plan of action is the plan that you write down that describes what you will need to do to achieve your goals. That means things like writing down your resources. That's what your coach does when he puts his game line together. You have to write down the people and talents and things that you have that will help you to accomplish your goals.

Next, you will have to research everything you can about your goals. Am I overwhelming you? It's really not hard. It just makes you think. Thinking is something that a lot of us don't do very often. One kid even told me once that all this thinking made his "brain hurt".

For instance, let's say that you want to become the greatest defenseman of all time. This is a big goal. Not impossible: just big. First write down your resources. Who do you know, what talents do you have and what things do you have at your disposal that will help you to achieve this goal. The "Who" might be your hockey director at your rink who was a defenseman on a NHL farm team or maybe there are hockey coaches around that can help you. Check out the web sites on the internet that might be able to put you in touch with your favorite defenseman.

Next what talents do you have? You know you skate really well and can skate as fast backward as forward. You play your position well on your team. You love to check. You are coachable. Things like that are talents.

Finally, what are the things that you have access to that can help you? Perhaps, you live five minutes from the rink. That's great! Maybe you also ref part-time. That definitely helps in your ice time. I think one of the best resources now for anyone is the World Wide Web. You can find anything on it and research it to your heart's content.

I don't want to go into too much detail about how to do all this. There are plenty of resources (books, videos, audiotapes, classes, etc.) in the market today that can teach you how to write down your goals and how to plan out your action steps. The main point I want to get across to you is that if you don't have a plan that is written down, you don't have a plan.

Off Ice Training Exercise

Write down some goals that you would like to achieve by
the end of the next hockey season.
Write down a goal that you would like to achieve within
the next five years.

If you don't design your own life plan, chances are you'll fall into someone else's plan. And guess what they have planned for you? Not much.

~ Jim Rohn ~

Chapter Four

Always Have a Plan "B"

We would all like to think that once we make a plan and we work towards that plan eventually the plan will work out. I'd like to tell you that your thinking is correct. I'd like to, but I can't. I've seen too many 'destined for greatness' hockey players not make it to "THE SHOW" as some call it. What happens when they don't make it and that's all they ever planned to do? No matter what you do sometimes things just don't pan out and the end result is that you have to rely on Plan "B". You do have a "Plan B" don't you?

Those who take the time to make a plan for their lives don't ever wish for Plan "B" to have to kick in but just in case, have a Plan "B".

What is a Plan "B"? Well, it's what you will do when Plan "A" doesn't work. Do you know why you have a Plan "B"? It's because you have to. Yeah, yeah, I hear you. You are saying 'I won't need a Plan "B" because my Plan "A" will work'. Great! Keep thinking that. There is a difference in the definition of confidence and stupidity. Look it up. Do you know another reason why you have a Plan "B"? You have a Plan "B" because it keeps you from being backed into a corner.

In hockey if Plan "A" is to get the puck then Plan "B" is to take the man. For example, if your opponent has the puck and you take a swipe at it and miss it you need to be in a position to impede the progress of your opponent. In hockey, as in life, people can't score if they are on their butts.

For example, let's say you are in your third year of college and you are playing collegiate hockey. Good for you. During a game you take a pass from a teammate and get checked into the boards and hear a loud crack. That crack was part of your anatomy. Yep, you just broke your wrist. Out for the rest of this season and the doctor isn't sure you will be back next season. What now? You *were* studying towards a major in school right? Now what? Plan "B".

I'm not trying to scare you into having another source for success and happiness in life but at least think about it. Take hockey out of the picture and start thinking about a Plan "B". Just in case.

Now, for the Life Lesson. In your life you will have situations that you will need to rely on a Plan "B". Life can't stop because your initial plan didn't work. You have to keep going. What are some examples of real life situations that require a Plan "B"?

Your Dad takes a promotion in another state and you will have to move far away from your friends and hockey team. Plan "B"? The college you were hoping to get into doesn't accept you and you have to go to another. Plan "B"? The job you were hoping to get straight out of college pays less than you thought it would. Plan "B"? You get that great promotion that you have been working really hard for only to find out that you have to move to the Antarctic. Plan "B"? The person you were planning to marry and spend the rest of your life with just said "no". Plan "B"?

Get the picture? Plan "B" is there to help you get past the hard spots so that you don't dwell on the negatives of a situation or an event. It allows you to regroup. What would happen to you in those situations if you didn't have another plan?

In my younger years I became interested in motorcycles. I loved the feel of the wind whipping through my hair and not being encumbered by a protective casing of metal. When I was finally able to buy my own, I loved the freedom that it gave me. One thing that most experienced riders will tell you, especially if you ride on busy streets, is always...always look for an exit or a way out. You know what that means? When you are riding you are constantly searching for a Plan "B". Yep. Just in case that other driver doesn't see you and runs the stop sign. Where do you go? What do you do? When you are on a motorcycle, just like when you are involved in living your life, it doesn't always help to say that it was the other guy's fault. Without a Plan "B" it won't make a difference whose fault it is. You may not be around long enough to set it straight.

Don't look at a Plan "B" as a failure mechanism. Look at it as a lifeboat. No one gets on a ship planning to have it sink. If it doesn't sink then great! If it does then you'll be around to tell about your harrowing experience when they interview you on the nightly news.

Off Ice Training Exercise

Write down two other things besides a sport that you would be interested in doing for a living. What interests you about them?

Action springs not from thought, but from a readiness
for responsibility.
~ Dietrich Bonhoeffer ~

CHAPTER FIVE

TAKE TIME TO SHARPEN YOUR SKATES

I was talking to a friend of mine the other day and he was telling me about how he ordered his young son his first pair of brand new hockey skates off the internet. He got a great deal! Now my friend is a wonderful guy but he knows absolutely nothing about hockey except for how to watch it on television. His son was just starting hockey and he was complaining that he could hardly stand up on the ice. Stopping was virtually impossible. I asked one simple question, "Mike, did you have his skates sharpened?". "Sharpened? Don't they come sharpened?" he asked.

That's just like life. We all get so excited about living it that we forget to slow down long enough to do what we have to do to really get the most out of it. I know most of you seasoned hockey players out there are laughing because you are thinking, "how can anyone not know about sharpening skates?" Well, when was the last time you didn't study for a test because you figured it would be pretty easy and it wasn't?

Taking the time to sharpen your skates is different from being prepared. Yes, it will help you to be prepared but sometimes you need to make the time just to stop and think about what you are doing or not doing. You can skate a whole season without re-sharpening your skates. But you would skate better if you took the time to sharpen them.

Take the time to do the things you need to do that will make you better. A couple of things come to mind. Why not sharpen your mind and start reading more? Why not sharpen your relationships with your family by listening and trying to understand them more? Why not sharpen your own physical conditioning by doing a little more off ice training or eating healthier?

The guys that really stand out in life are the ones that are willing to stop and "sharpen their skates". Do a little more than the other guy is willing to do. Think of your favorite professional hockey players. What makes them stand out to you? Is it because they do everything the same as everyone else? What makes them different?

Off Ice Training Exercise

Write down someone whom you admire and then write down what you think they do that makes them that way.

I don't care how good you play, you can find somebody who can beat you, and I don't care how bad you play, you can find somebody you can beat.
~ Harvey Penick ~

CHAPTER SIX

EVENTUALLY YOU WILL HAVE TO TRYOUT FOR THE TEAM

I remember my son's first tryout for a competitive hockey team. He had never had to "tryout" before. He had always been on house teams. Getting goaltenders on house teams was really difficult. Getting a good goalie was next to impossible. His teams always welcomed him with open arms. This tryout for a travel team was entirely different.

He was going up against some of the best goaltenders in the area. He was really out of his comfort zone. He kept asking us, "what if they are better than me?" and "what if I play lousy during the tryouts?"

Life is like that. You may be the most popular kid in your school right now but things will change. You won't always be the tallest or the smartest or the best looking or the most popular. At one time or another you may find yourself in a group of people just as good as you. Think of the best hockey players your age that you know. Now, imagine having to play against a whole team of them. Do you know what the name of that team is when you get older? It's called the NHL.

Okay, so you aren't going to be the best or the brightest all of the time. What do you do then? Well, you have two choices. You can tuck your tail between your legs and go home. You wouldn't believe how many people do that! Or you can take a deep breath and go for it! When I say 'go for it' I mean just do the best that you can do. You can't control if you win or lose. You *can* control whether or not you give 100%. If you don't make the team then at least learn from it. That way your time hasn't been a total waste.

Back to my son. He didn't make that team. Being the kind of kid he is (and you should be too) he called the coach up and asked what he needed to work on to make the team next year.

Here's another story. A friend of mine was asked by an USA Olympic Hockey Team Scout to tryout for a position on the 1980 USA Hockey Team. He was given a slip of paper with instructions and told where to go on a particular day. Well, it so happens that on that same day there was a big party that all of his friends were going to. He had to make a decision. Would he go to the tryout and risk being cut or would he go to the party and have a great time? He chose the safest thing. He chose the party. The rest is history. The USA won the gold medal that year in ice hockey. My friend watched it on television. Tryouts can be tough but they won't kill you. My friend will tell you that trying and failing is not as bad as not trying and regretting it for the rest of your life.

In life you will have tryouts. Whether they will be for teams or jobs. Sometimes tryouts are for "the girl of your dreams" or the right to drive. Adults go through tryouts all the time. They tryout when they want a new car or house and they have to fill out a credit application. They tryout when they go in to ask their boss for a raise. They tryout when they go for their yearly physical. Practically everything you do in life is a tryout. Remember that. If you make it - Great! If you don't, find out what you can do to improve and do it! And for heaven's sake keep trying out.

Off Ice Training Exercise

Write a list of things that you will have to tryout for in
the next couple of years.

T hank God for competition. When our competitors
upset our plans or outdo our designs, they open infinite
possibilities of our own work to us.
~ Gil Atkinson ~

CHAPTER SEVEN

SOMEONE ELSE WANTS YOUR SPOT ON THE TEAM

Okay, you've gone through tryouts and you have made the team. Congratulations! Now you are at practice. Your coach blows the whistle and assigns you to the power play line. He explains a simple overload system then dumps the puck into the corner and off you go with your bad self. Wait! You weren't paying attention. What's your responsibility? Where are you supposed to be? Tweet! Hey #16 (that's you) you're out! # 12, take his place. It happens that quickly.

You skate off and watch while #12 performs the overload effortlessly. What the heck happened? One minute you were King of the Ice, the next minute you are watching someone else play your position better than you. That's when it hits you. You can be replaced! Oh no! Being on a team is one continual tryout!

Welcome to Life. Just because you make a team doesn't mean you get to relax and quit trying. I've seen a lot of adults do that very thing. They finish school and they quit learning. They get a job and they do just enough to get by. You can't do that in hockey and you can't do that in life. Ask anyone who has been to the top. Sure, it's hard to get there but they will all tell you that it is harder to stay there.

Years ago in hockey, goaltenders didn't wear a facemask. Can you imagine? Then one day after getting hit way too often in the face Jacques Plante made himself a facemask. It was really scary looking. Kind of like the character with the goalie mask in the horror movie. It protected him some but it still hurt like heck when the puck hit him. Now he is remembered in hockey history as the first goaltender to wear a facemask. Through the years other goaltenders started to improve on the mask until you have what we have today. What would have happened if people just decided that Jacques Plante's mask was good enough?

How about Wayne Gretzky, the "Great One" of hockey? What if he relaxed after he made the NHL? What kind of records would he have racked up? It will be a long time before someone beats Gretzky's records.

What you have to remember is this. No matter how good you are and no matter how liked you are ...someone will come along and try to beat you at your own game. You have to keep improving yourself. That way it takes them longer to catch up to you! Be the one to set the standard and then continue setting new standards. Make it hard for someone to out do you. Have fun but don't relax when it comes time to showing people why you are the best.

Don't hate the guy trying to out do you. Your competition is not to be hated. It's there for a reason. Competition makes you better. The better the competition, the better you have to be to beat it. It makes you strive for more. It makes you skate a little faster, focus more intently and try a little harder.

I think of competition like a sharpening stone for your skates. If you only rubbed your skate blade along something soft all the time it would turn dull. It takes something hard to sharpen a skate. If you want to be dull then turn away from competition. If you want to be sharp and cut through life then you will need competition to keep yourself sharp.

If it weren't for competition we wouldn't have sports of any kind. The whole objective in sports is to be better than you started out being and the only way you can be better than you are is for someone else to come along and challenge you. Your attitude towards competition is what makes you who you are as an athlete and as a person. Welcome competition, rise to its challenge and overcome it.

Off Ice Training Exercise

Make a list of things that you would like to be considered
the BEST at doing.

In the practice of tolerance, one's enemy is the best teacher.
~Dalai Lama~

Chapter Eight

You Won't Always Like Your Coach

I know, you're saying "what do you mean I won't like my coach?!" That's great. I'm glad that you like your coach. Coaches should be likeable people. Some of my best friends are coaches. But that doesn't erase the fact that if you stay in hockey for any length of time you might just get a coach that you don't like. Or worse yet, the coach doesn't like you! You might as well hang up your skates. Yep, go ahead and put a 3x5 index card up on the used equipment sale bulletin board. Your hockey career is over.

Hey, wake up! I'm kidding. Just because you don't like your coach doesn't mean it's the end of your hockey career. It does pose some interesting challenges. Life is like that! You knew I was going to say that didn't you?

Ask yourself. Did you really like all of your teachers? Did you like all the kids in your class? Sometimes you may have even found yourself disliking your own parents! What is wrong with you? Nothing is wrong with you. Or maybe you were thinking there was something wrong with them. Well, that's a viable option. Let's blame it on them. NOT! Life is very interesting. And the things that make life interesting are the different types of people that are in it.

Now, let's get back to your coach. Your coach is important. Coaches are supposed to help make you a better player. Coaches should be fair and consistent. Coaches should be looking out for the player's and team's best interest. It isn't always going to be like that in life. Just like it won't always be that way in hockey.

Sometimes you get a coach whose main emphasis is on winning no matter what it takes. And in hockey I have seen the "no matter what it takes" translate into checking from behind, slew footing players, hooking, tripping, etc.

Sometimes you get a coach who yells and screams himself hoarse every game at you (or it sure seems like he is directing it at you). Sometimes you may even get a coach whose son plays on the team and plays every other line out while everyone else sits the bench for two line changes.

Now, for the Life Lesson. In life you will get people who will take the place of your coach. Like your boss. Right now your coach has nothing to do with your ability to make money. As a matter of fact you are probably paying to play. But as you get older you may find yourself in a situation where your coach at your job (the boss) is a real tyrant. You may love what you do for a living. You may love that great salary. You are actually getting paid for doing what you love. BUT, you can't stand your boss! What to do, what to do? Do you quit? Do you whine and complain to your co-workers? Do you write anonymous notes about him and post them by the water cooler? I don't know, you tell me. What would be the best thing to do?

Let's think this through together. If you learned the Life Lesson from hockey, you learned that:

1) complaining to your teammates doesn't help at all

2) quitting probably will only hurt you and slow down (if not end) your hockey career and

3) coaches, like bosses, are not perfect. They are human, just like you.

The best thing to do is to realize that you have a job to do while you are there. Do your job to the best of your ability. Do what you can to be a team player and if all that doesn't work then you start looking for another "team" to play on. But remember this, in life as in hockey, bad mouthing the coach of the team that you are on only makes you look stupid for being on the team in the first place. Do your job and look for a trade, don't try to second guess or bad mouth the coach or your boss.

Let me give you an example from a friend of mine. My friend was offered a full college scholarship to play for a college hockey team. He was very good. Not because he said so, everyone that knew him said he was very good. Anyway, he received this scholarship and began college.

My friend played goaltender. There were four goal-tenders that made the team. One was a senior, one was junior and the other two were freshmen. My friend was one of the freshmen. As I said, my friend was very good. Actually, better than the other goaltenders on the team. He thought he should have started. His coach thought otherwise.

My friend at that time didn't know the importance of being a team player or seeing the big picture or being patient so he quit. Right out of the blue. He quit. He didn't like his coach and he quit. Looking back he regrets that decision. It ended his hockey career.

Your coach and your boss may never notice you. They may not notice how much time you put in or how hard you work. Someone will notice you if you always give 100%. Maybe it will be your teammates. Maybe it will be a scout. Make sure that you are doing the things that will get you noticed in a positive way. Most of all, you need to make sure that *you* notice the things that you are doing.

Let me give you a little hint. The next time you are trying out for a team try introducing yourself to the coach before the tryout and tell him that you are his new starting defenseman (or whatever position you play). If nothing else he will know who you are. Remember to back your mouth up with your playing.

A few years ago, some friends and I went to this great outdoor concert. It was a band that we had grown up listening to and we knew all the words to their songs. I was so excited about this concert. My friends were excited about the concert too, until we sat down on the blanket that we had spread out on the grass to relax and listen to this band. That's when the mosquitoes showed up.

It wasn't a swarm of mosquitoes. It was a few mosquitoes but enough to be a little bothersome. One particular friend thought these mosquitoes were terrible. From the time the band started to play until their last encore she complained the entire time about the mosquitoes. When we finally got in the car to go home and started to talk about the concert she mentioned in a disappointed voice that the band had not played several of their biggest hits.

The rest of us had to tell her that they had in fact played those songs. She had been so obsessed about the mosquitoes that she had totally missed the concert. My point is this. Sometimes we get so involved in the little things that are irritating us in our lives that we miss the really important things.

When your coach is yelling at you about something you are doing or not doing on the ice, remember that he is doing what he thinks is best for you as a player and for the team. Don't tune out the message because you don't like the way it is being delivered. Separate yourself from the voice and hear the message.

<u>Another helpful hint</u>. Whenever your coach is talking to you, on the ice or on the bench on in the dressing room stop what you are doing and look him straight in the eye. Pay attention, nod your head and listen. Do NOT say "I know". If he thought you knew he wouldn't be telling you again. If you don't understand what he is saying to you, ask a question. This will go a long way towards how the coach perceives you.

Remember that the people in power are in power for a reason. Try to see the big picture whenever you can and don't make any quick decisions when you don't have to. As a hockey player, student, family member or an employee you won't always be able to the see "the big picture" but you won't have to if you make yourself a part of it!

Off Ice Training Exercise

Make a list of the people who in your life (past, present
or future) have caused you or may cause you to have to
make a difficult decision.
Write down how you will handle those decisions.

There are four ways, and only four ways, in which we have contact with the world. We are evaluated and classified by these four contacts:
what we do, how we look, what we say, and how we say it.
~ Dale Carnegie ~

Chapter Nine

In Hockey, There is a Lot of Communication

Communication: what a great word. Have you ever thought what it means to communicate? I'm doing it right now with you and we can't even see each other. It means that I can transfer a message to you. It takes at least two people to communicate. There has to be someone who is sending out the communication and someone who is receiving the communication. Otherwise it would be like sending up a flare when you are lost and no one seeing it. Wasted flare.

I love it when they put microphones on the ice and you can hear the players. You can hear how they are talking to each other and calling out each other's names for a play. They all have a common goal and that is to win the game. All of their communication is slanted in that direction. Occasionally, communication takes the form of a verbal fight but that's part of the game too.

In life off the ice, communication is very important also. Have you ever tried to go through an entire day not communicating in some form or fashion? Communication doesn't just mean talking. It could be writing on paper or via e-mail. It could also mean body language. Think about it. If you ask a friend of yours what he thinks about something and he shrugs his shoulders hasn't he just communicated with you?

In my life away from the hockey rinks I used to be a corporate recruiter and trainer. You know one of those people that help other people find the job of their dreams. Well, sometimes. Anyway, when I interviewed people I would watch to see how they communicated. Did they look at me while I was talking to them? Did they strum their fingers nervously when I asked them a question? What exactly did the rolling of their eyes mean when I asked them about their last job?

People can tell a lot about you just by listening or watching or reading the way you communicate. Here is a hockey example. What if during a game your coach stands behind the bench and doesn't do anything? He doesn't speak, he doesn't move his hands, he doesn't even nod his head. What are you going to do as a team? Does he even need to be there?

If you are a poor communicator it's as if you didn't exist. Worse yet, it could make your life miserable. Why do I say that? Because your friends or players on your team or people at your work will misunderstand what you mean about things. If you are constantly having to say to people "I didn't mean it that way", or "You didn't hear me right" or "I never said that" you need to stop and take a long look at how you are communicating.

Recently a word has been reintroduced into the English language with an entirely different meaning. It is one word but it speaks volumes. The word is 'whatever'. Have you ever heard that word? Its original definition is 'everything or anything, no matter what'. Now, more than ever, you hear it said with a rolling of the eyes. However, now when you hear the word spoken it usually takes on the meaning of "what you are saying isn't important to me and I don't care about what you are talking about or you." What a terrible word to say to someone. I have heard this word come out of players' mouths to their coaches, their parents and to their teammates. If this person was interviewing for his dream job you can bet he wouldn't get it.

Think about the words that come out of your mouth. You should never use a word that you don't know the meaning of and always make sure that your emphasis on the word is not negative.

Communication also deals with attitude. It seems that there is always one player on a hockey team that is more negative than the rest. You know him, he's the one that says "we're doing that drill again?" kind of in a whiney voice. Or he says "this is stupid, why do we have to wear our travel suits when we are just going to a rink in the same town". Zig Ziglar, a famous motivational speaker, has a great saying. It is, "your attitude will determine your altitude". He is right. How high you go in life will be determined a great deal by your attitude.

My husband, who is a Master's Level Hockey Coach, has always told me that he would rather pick a player who has a great attitude and a little bit of talent for a team than a really talented player with a lousy attitude. The lousy attitude hurts the team. A player with a great attitude is willing to work to become a better player and a better teammate.

Bosses know that too. Remember that the way you communicate is with your whole body not just your mouth.

Another form of communication is listening. That's right. You didn't know that did you? Did you know that people think that you are great at communicating if you just listen more intently to what they have to say?

Try this experiment. Next time one of your parents is trying to make a point to you, stop whatever you are doing, look at them while they are talking to you and listen carefully at the message they are trying to get across to you. Don't interrupt, just listen. You will be amazed at the results. Be careful of your facial expressions. Don't roll your eyes or smirk or have this look of 'are you done yet?' on your face. Look interested. Your parents won't be around forever. One day you will miss hearing their voices. Pay attention. Listen. Learn to communicate without saying a word. When people feel like you are listening, they feel like you care about them and the ideas that they have to share with you.

Off Ice Training Exercise

Watch how people communicate without speaking.
Look at yourself in a mirror and try to communicate with your
facial expressions. What kind of communicator are you?

You may be deceived if you trust too much,
but you will live in torment if you don't trust enough.
~ Frank Crane ~

CHAPTER TEN

YOU HAVE TO TRUST YOUR TEAMMATES

When you watch a really good hockey game you see a lot of trust out on the ice. When you watch a game where players are playing positional hockey you see how the trust factor comes into play. Watch a game where a player doesn't leave his position to go after the man with the puck. He trusts that his teammate will take care of that and then he will be in the right position to make himself available for a pass.

Watch a goaltender on a team with really good defense. The goaltender trusts his defensemen to stop the man with the puck before it gets to him and his defensemen trusts the goaltender to stop the puck if it gets past them.

A team has to trust the coach. They have to know that he knows what he is doing and that he sees the game from another angle that they can't see. The coach has to trust his team. He has to know that they have come prepared to play and that they have listened during the many hours of practice. The fans come to the game trusting that the players will show up to entertain them. The players trust that the fans will show up to cheer them on.

You have to have a lot of trust on and off the ice. What exactly is trust? The dictionary defines trust as being 'a confidence or faith in a person or thing'. What type of person has no trust in anyone? A very lonely person. You have to trust other people.

I see people all the time that don't really trust anyone. They say they do but they don't. You can tell who these people are by just watching them. They check and re-check what other people do. For instance, you are heading into the local bookstore and you pull on the door and it is locked. You notice then that the sign says that the store will open in five minutes. You turn around to go back to your car to wait and another guy comes up heading towards the door. You say to him "the doors locked, it will open in five minutes". He nods his head like he under-stands you and then proceeds to try to open the door any-way. Why did he do that? He doesn't trust what you are telling him. Why doesn't he? Maybe because he doesn't know you or maybe you looked like you didn't know what you were talking about or maybe he is that way with everyone.

In all my years as a recruiter I have studied a lot about human nature and why people do certain things. Why people don't trust others is a really deep subject. A subject too deep for this book. All you have to know is that in life you have to trust people. You should want to trust people. It makes life nicer and easier to go through.

I have also found that people who don't trust other peo-ple usually think that if they trust other people they are showing a weakness in themselves. They have this idea that as long as they don't have to trust in anyone else they must be strong. In reality, it takes a strong person to trust other people. You have to be strong to let go of your fear of losing control of a situation. People that are smarter than me in this area have told me that people who fear the loss of control really are never happy. They are constantly having to work at controlling everything in their life. That takes a lot of energy. That energy could be spent on better things.

When you allow yourself to trust other people then you let go of your fear of being inadequate. That means that you know that whatever happens, happens. Believe me, many of us spend entirely too much time thinking that people are constantly judging us and that everything we do and say is being watched. The people around you have better things to do with their lives than to watch your every move. And if they live their life in order to catch you doing something less than perfect they are the ones with the problem.

You have to know that trusting people is a sign of strength and not weakness. It's pretty vain for you to think that you and only you know how to do something, and that no one else can do it better than you can.

Now, I'm not saying that if someone burns you that you keep on trusting them. Gomer Pyle, a television character from way back when, used to say in his nasally southern drawl, "Fool me once, shame on you. Fool me twice, shame on me". There are people out there that can't and shouldn't be trusted. And you shouldn't feel the least bit bad about steering clear of them. Those are people who need professional help and you are not the professional to give it to them. I'm saying that you need to trust people until they give you a reason not to.

With this is mind I have to also tell you that the person you need to trust the most is yourself. Listen to your own intuition. That's that little voice inside you saying "hey, don't do that!" Many people trust other people but don't trust themselves. If *you* don't trust yourself why should I trust you? I find that the best way to gauge whether or not to trust someone is to ask myself "what are their intentions". If you stop somewhere and ask a nice looking older man working out in his yard for directions and he gives them to you, his intentions must be pretty good. I don't think he gets his jollies by giving bad directions intentionally to lost strangers. Do you?

You need to do the same thing for yourself. When you need to make a decision on what to do and you aren't sure whether or not to do it, then ask yourself, "what is my intention towards doing this thing?" If your answer is a positive one in which you are trying to help someone or it is for a good cause or you are doing something good then continue. However, if your answer is because you want to embarrass someone or you want to break curfew or you are going to do something that inevitably will not be construed as good then stop! Your intuition in trying to tell you something. Trust yourself.

Have you ever sat through one of those scary movies where one of the characters hears a noise upstairs and grabs the flashlight and starts heading towards the noise? Are you like me? Are you saying in your head, "don't do that, that's stupid, you're about to be killed, GET OUT OF THE HOUSE!!"

There will be times in your life that you are that person and everyone around you is yelling for you to get out of the house (or situation) and you just keep going. When a lot of people whose opinions you respect are telling you the same thing then just stop and listen to them. Ask yourself 'what are their intentions' and then decide for yourself what is the best thing to do. Just remember, in order to do this you must stop, take the time to think, ask the "all important" question about intentions and then trust in yourself to make the right decision. Just make sure that you are being truthful with yourself. William Shakespeare said it best, "To thine own self be true".

Off Ice Training Exercise

Write down the names of the people you trust.
Now, write down what their intentions are towards you.

There are no exceptions to the rule that everybody
likes to be an exception to the rule.
~ Charles Osgood ~

CHAPTER ELEVEN

YOU HAVE TO KNOW THE RULES

Hockey is a great sport to play and to watch. Since I am not a great skater I have to admit I enjoy watching it more than I do playing it. When you are watching a game you can get caught up in the rhythm of the game. The puck gets dropped at the face-off and the game takes on a life of its own. The puck glides down the ice and is picked up by a player who makes a perfect pass to his teammate. Another pass and then another and then a shot! The goaltender makes the save and sends the puck out towards one of his own players who then makes a beautiful pass to another teammate and the game continues.

The players exchange places on the bench barely noticed and the game goes on. Occasionally there is a whistle or a score but the game still has a life of its own. What keeps this game running so smoothly? The Rules. Everyone out there knows the rules. Who can and can't go where. Where the face-offs are and aren't. How many men can be on the ice?

That's life. Anyone can watch a game of hockey. Not everyone can play it. Whether or not you enjoy life is whether or not you learn the rules and get in the game. Some people try to play the game without knowing what the rules are. You've seen them. They keep getting called for being off-sides. Eventually they will get frustrated and quit playing.

Learn the rules if you want to play in the game of life. Everyone starts out with their own set of rules for their life. Sometimes their rules work. Sometimes they don't. If you want your life to be a great life then you have to make sure that you are playing by the right set of rules. You can't play hockey with a set of rules from baseball. Learn the rules. Here are five very basic rules to start you out.

1. <u>The game starts on time</u>. This means that you came along just at the right time. You weren't late and you weren't early. Your game started when you got here. It also means that once you are here you can't just drag your feet thinking that everyone will wait for you. Get in the game!

2. <u>The whistles are there for a reason</u>. The different whistles that you hear in your life might be warning signs or signs that tell you that you need to stop doing what you are doing and change direction. The whistles can also tell you that you are not following the rules and if you are not careful you can be put in a place that you will need to sit out and only watch the game being played instead of playing in it. Bad place to be. Listen for the whistles and stop whatever you are doing when you hear them.

3. <u>You can't skate on the ice until the Zamboni is done</u>. Patience is a virtue. Sometimes in your life you will have all this energy and want to make a difference but you will have to wait. The surface isn't ready yet for you to do your thing. Get dressed, tape your stick, wait on the bench and then when the surface is ready for you, do your thing and do it really well.

4. <u>You can't skate any faster than your legs will carry you.</u> You are responsible for your life. No one can make you be what you don't want to be. Someone else can buy you the top of the line skates but you can't skate any faster than your own legs will allow you to. You have to want to. Same in life. Your coach may be the greatest coach of all time. Your teammates may be candidates for the Hockey Hall of Fame. They aren't you. YOU have to do something to get you where you want to be.

5. <u>You have to wear a uniform</u>. There are rules in hockey instructing players what they can and can't wear during a game. That's so that everyone can tell what team they play for and can identify the player. Make sure you dress in a way that will identify you to people. If you want to be known as a slob, dress like a slob. If you want to be known as successful, then dress for success. Your choice. But remember, in hockey and in life, if you aren't dressed right you don't play.

That's five basic rules. There are a lot more that you can learn as you go.

Off Ice Training Exercise

What do you want people to think of you?
How will you need to dress in order for that to happen?

Good work habits help develop an internal tough-
ness and a self-confident attitude that will sustain you
through every adversity and temporary discouragement.
~ Paul J. Fleyer ~

Chapter Twelve

Playing Great Hockey is A Lot of Work

Welcome to by favorite chapter. Why? Because I love watching people do what they love to do and make good money doing it. These people stand out from the rest of the crowd. They love doing what they do so much that they don't even consider it working!

What makes these people so different? They decided early on what they loved to do and then they applied a good strong work ethic to it. What's a work ethic? Well a work ethic is the way someone works. Do you put 85% into your work or do you give 100% all the time? Do you show up for work on time or five minutes late everyday? Do you do just enough to get by?

Let's look at it from a hockey standpoint. Have you ever seen a player 'coast' towards the puck? How about a player that makes wide circles instead of stopping and going the other way? Have you played with a player who every time he was hit crumpled to the ground in agony (a little dramatic don't you think)? How about a player that is so afraid of getting hit that he won't go into the corners and he'll pass the puck to no one in particular instead of taking the hit? Ever seen a puck hog? Ever had a teammate that didn't give 100% in the practices but expected to play in the games an equal amount of time as those players that gave 100%? (Coaches know that you practice like you play). Ever had a teammate badmouth other players and the coaches behind their backs? Ever seen a hockey player take something out of some other player's bag that didn't belong to him?

What kind of work ethic do you think those types of players have? What types of adults do you think they will grow up to be? Would you want that type of player working with you or for you? Are you that type of player?

A good work ethic comes from years of practice. That's right. Regardless of whether or not you are a good hockey player the work habits you are establishing now will remain with you the rest of your life. If you think that maybe you have been slacking off, then make up your mind not to be that way. You are the only one that can determine your work ethic. You may see a bad example in those around you but you can determine to have a good strong work ethic.

A very important thing to remember about a work ethic is that it is an internal thing. You can't just do it on the outside. You have to have the same work ethic regardless of whether your coach or boss or parent is watching over you or you are all alone doing what you are doing. You have to know that doing what is right all the time is reward in itself.

I once watched a movie called "Defending Your Life" in which a man dies and has to give reasons why he did some of the things he did in his life. His whole life had been recorded. If your whole life were being recorded would you act any differently? If your answer is yes, then you need to rethink the way you are acting now.

Once a strong work ethic is in place then you can determine what it is that you want to do in your life and be a success. Let's see what your work ethic rating is right now. Ask yourself these questions and answer with true or false.

1. Whenever I am given a job to do I complain about doing it and then do just enough of it to get it over with. Example, stuffing clean clothes into a dirty laundry hamper or shoving everything under the bed instead of folding them and putting them up. In hockey terms, during a skating drill when you are supposed to skate all the way up to the blue line you stop a foot short and head back or you make a wide circle past it and coast back.

2. I very rarely volunteer to do anything that would help my family out.

3. I expect to get paid for everything that I do or I won't do it.

4. I think that if no one else can see it then it doesn't matter if I pick it up.

5. I wait until I am told several times to do something before I do it.

6. I use the words "in a second", "give me a minute" and "I'll do it later" whenever I am asked to do something.

7. I have lied saying that I have completed a job when I haven't.

8. I work harder when I know someone is watching me.

If you answered true to any of these questions you really need to take a good strong look at the kind of person you are training yourself to be. If you said true to all of these questions you need to ask yourself how and why your family even puts up with you anymore.

Off Ice Training Exercise

Write down three things that you could do to improve
your work ethic.

We herd sheep, we drive cattle, we lead people.
Lead me, follow me, or get out of my way.
~ George S. Patton ~

Chapter Thirteen

Lead, Follow or Get Out of the Way!

Have you ever wondered what it takes to be a team player?
It's some of the things that we have already talked about.

- Knowing that it won't always be perfect.
- You won't always like each other but you have to get along.
- Sometimes there will be competition within the team.
- You must be prepared.
- You have to trust your teammates.
- You have to know the rules.
- You have to communicate.
- You have to have a good strong work ethic.

Successful teams must have a good leader. Not everyone can be a leader at the same time. There must be followers for the leader to lead. Successful leaders lead by example.

What happens to a team if the leader doesn't set a good example?

Does this mean that once you are a leader you are always a leader? No. Does this mean that once you are a follower you are always a follower? No. After all, where do you think we get good leaders? They are good followers first.

In order to become a good leader you must possess certain qualities. The first and most important is that you must be willing to follow someone else when you are not the leader. Good leaders don't play the "it's my ball and if I can't play my way then I'm going home and taking my ball with me" game. Good leaders do what is best for the team.

In order to be a good follower you must know everything the leader knows and also watch and follow the example he sets for you. You must also make sure that the leader has everything they need to lead. A good follower is also ready to be the leader when he is called upon to do so.

What a good follower is NOT...is a pushover. They follow because it is not their time to lead. Otherwise they would be leading. Please don't mistake a good follower as someone who blindly follows someone or something no matter what. Followers are people who are there to provide the strength and stability necessary on a team. They help to achieve the goals of the team.

Occasionally, there are those people who are neither leaders nor followers. They are like bad spots on the ice. They are there to trip the team up. They are the 'one man shows'. They complain when the team wins because they didn't get enough ice time. They complain when the team loses because they didn't get enough ice time. The only thing they do really well is complain. It is never their fault;

it is always someone else's fault. For lack of a better term, I call these players "quicksand".

It doesn't matter how good of a leader or follower you are these players are quicksand. And if you start to hang out with them you'll be stuck in the same quicksand. Now I don't know much about quicksand but I do know this. You can't skate on it! And neither can they. Eventually, as the competition becomes tougher, they work themselves out of a team and/or organization.

Think of your team as a team of sled dogs. There is one leader and lots of followers. It can only work that way. Remember also that the lead dog has to set the pace and pull harder than every one else.

In life outside of hockey you'll come into contact with hundreds of each type. Learn from the leaders, support the followers and avoid at all costs the quicksand.

Off Ice Training Exercise

Take some time and think about what type of person
you are.
Are you a leader, a follower or quicksand?
If you don't like what you are then think about how you
can change.

Experience is not what happens to a man;
it is what a man does with what happens to him.
~ Aldous Huxley ~

CHAPTER FOURTEEN

YOU HAVE TO REVIEW THE GAME TAPES

After the game the coach may get the team together to review the game tape. You'll love watching this tape if you played position and passed accurately and scored whenever you got near the net or made some really good saves. Everyone loves to see himself when they are playing well. It's when you have played lousy that you hate sitting through the game tape.

Why do coaches make you do that? Because life will make you do that. There will be times during your life that in order for you to get better you will have to look at what you did wrong and the only way to do that is to watch the game tape. In life, that may mean sitting down with a friend that can "replay" the scene for you. It may mean just taking time out and reliving the moment.

That's hard to do because you always want to make excuses for why you acted in a particular way. I've seen that in game meetings when a player refuses to admit that it was his fault that the other team scored because he was out of position. He gives excuses as to why he was out of position but in the end the tape says it all. Your life will do the same thing. It won't matter that you "thought" you were doing the right thing or that you "thought" no one would ever find out about it or that you "thought" what you were doing was okay because there were a bunch of other people doing it. In the end it all boils down to the "game tape" of your life. What did it look like when everything was said and done.

Whenever you feel like your life isn't going the way you had planned it to go, stop. Rewind the tape and take a good hard look at it. Don't look at the tape searching for the good things you did, look for the mistakes. The times that you were out of position. The times that you dragged your feet when you should have been going hard for the puck. Stop making excuses and find out what you did that can be corrected and then correct it. The tape is not there to condemn you. It's there to help you.

When the coach points out to you what you did wrong are you saying to yourself, "he's just picking on me because he doesn't like me", or "he doesn't know what he's talking about". Instead, listen and understand that he wants to help you become the best player you can be because it's good for the team and its good for you. It's the same in life. You want to be the best you that you can be. It's not enough to be half of what you can be. You have to think along the lines of being everything and more than you can be. Push yourself to excel.

Have you ever been in a situation where you did or said something that you wish you could take back but it was too late? That's when you rewind the game tape. Each play in hockey (and in life) follows another. A play just doesn't happen. Rewind your game tape to the point where you think the whole thing started and then rewind it a little more. Find out where the initial situation started. What caused you to say or do what you said or did that you regret now?

Once you find out what that is then try really hard not to do it again. I find that it helps to write it down. Not for the whole world to see. Just for you. Something like, "when I get around Stephanie she makes me nervous and I say really stupid things about other people that embarrass them." Then write down your solution to this. It may be, "when Stephanie is around I have to not talk about anyone else but myself. That way if I say something stupid I only embarrass myself." That's a start. See how the game tape works?

Off Ice Training Exercise

Write down something you did recently that you regret.
Rewind the game tape on it and figure out what you
could have done instead.

"The best thing about sports is the sense of community and shared emotion it can create"
—-Bob Costas

Chapter Fifteen

Being Part of Something Bigger

What makes athletes stay in a sport long after they have made the big time and long after they have proven themselves? I had asked myself that very question when I watched Wayne Gretzky skate around the ice at his last NHL game as a player. There he was "the Great One" skating around the ice waving to the crowd with this sad smile on his face. I thought to myself, "he's a legend, he's the player every young hockey player dreams about being, he's worth millions of dollars, why is he so sad?"

I received my answer one night while I was sitting in the stands watching my son practice with his team. I had the good fortune of sitting beside a very successful NHL coach (don't you envy me?). We started talking about the most important thing about sports and the Life Lessons that players get out of it.

I have to tell you that some of the best things I have learned in my life have come from coaches (famous and not-so-famous, someone else's and my own). They have a different way of looking at things. They see the big picture a lot of the time. Maybe it's because they have to focus on what is going on. I don't know why some of them are so wise, they just are.

In any case, this coach started telling me about the things he remembered while playing and coaching hockey. He didn't remember the scores of the games that they had won or lost, what he remembered was the feeling he had when they won or when they lost. It's the feelings you have when you see the rest of your team celebrating after a big win. And it's the feelings you have when you see everyone on the team nearly in tears after an upset that ends the season.

That was it! That's why players love to play. Sure, it may look like they play for the money and the fame and all the other great things that come with being a great athlete. But, really when it all boils down to it, they play the game for the same reasons they played it when they were 10 years old. They play because they love the feeling of being part of something bigger. It's about putting aside the individual's needs and wants and doing what is best for the life of the team. They love the team mentality. The 'all for one and one for all' feeling that you get when you are on a team.

That's why old athletes never die they just become coaches, managers, scouts, and a hundred other things that will allow them to still be part of a team. That's why corporate America seeks out people who have been team players before. They know that with a team mentality they often, more than not, make great employees.

My husband still plays hockey. Our son calls it "old man's hockey", my husband prefers to call it "hall of fame hockey". Whatever name you give to it, it's great fun to watch! Here are a bunch of guys that played hockey when they were younger. Some played it in high school and some in college and some even made it to the NHL. Some are no-so-good skaters; others skate with reckless abandon. What all these players have in common is their love of the game. You have to love the game to play it at this age when you are not getting paid to play. *You are paying to play*. You play late at night when ice time is less expensive and very few family members can make it to cheer you on. They play this game because they love the high fives from their teammates when they score. They play this game because they love the feeling of sacrificing themselves as a human shield to stop a puck headed straight for the open corner of the net. They play the entire game laughing, trying not to take themselves too seriously and breathing hard.

At the end of a game they all skate off smiling. They look like 10 year old kids in 40+ year old bodies. This same scene goes on all around America in virtually every rink that hockey is played on. Late at night after the kids are asleep. A "hall of fame" team steps out onto the ice and becomes young again. It's like watching men go through some time portal, only to come out on the other side as young kids. For that brief moment in time they don't remember that they aren't as fast as they used to be. They don't remember that their shot is not as hard or as accurate. They don't even remember that they have to get up in the morning and go back to work. All they know when they step out on the ice is that they are part of a team.

Now, for the Life Lesson. Being part of a team is about sharing your life with other people. Not being part of a team is like having a really great secret and not being able to tell anyone. You can't even tell anyone that you have a great secret that you can't tell them.

Being part of a team, whether it is a family, a hockey team, or a construction team means that everyone makes a difference. I have found also that when you combine all the talents of the people on a team you come out with much more than what each individual team member brings into it. What does that mean? It means synergy. Synergy means that $1+1 = 3$ or more. It means that when you put people together they are stronger, smarter, more inventive, more ambitious, and more successful than they would normally be as individuals. Team adds a special kind of magic to whatever you are doing.

When I think of a team I think of when the U.S.A. Men's Olympic Hockey Team won the gold in 1980. They weren't even supposed to get that far in the Olympics. Something happened to them that made them create a miracle on ice. It was because they were a team. They were all thinking about the same thing, they were all trying to accomplish the same goal. And they were able to do it through this 'all for one and one for all' mentality. No one person was more important that anyone else. They were going to do it together or they weren't going to be able to do it at all.

Now, a question for you. If you have ever seen the video of that team winning the gold medal in the Olympics can you tell me who they played and what the final score was? I have to be honest with you, I can't tell you. I can tell you though how they reacted to it. They were jumping up and down on the ice, hugging each other, smiling, crying, and most of all creating a memory that will stay with them long after they have hung up their skates. They will be able to tell you who was on the ice with them and the feeling they felt when they heard the crowds chanting, "U….S….A". Those gold medal winners can tell you how it felt to be part of a team. And I can pretty much guarantee you that they wouldn't trade that feeling for anything in the world.

Remember that being part of a team is important. There are times in your life when you will want to be alone. You will want to use those times to think about what you want to be, where you want to go and how you want to accomplish those things in your life. When you are finished being by yourself then you are going to want to have a team there with you to share those experiences.

There is never a better measure of what a person is than
what he does when
he is absolutely free to choose.
~ William M. Bulger ~

Chapter Sixteen

And The Game Goes On

Well, here we are. You have actually read a book that might help you in your life. It wasn't a book designed to give you all the answers. That part is going to be up to you. It was designed to make you start thinking about your life. I hope that by writing it along the lines of hockey that you were able to relate to it more. There are a lot of good Life Lessons to learn in hockey if you are willing to learn them.

I have always believed in having heroes. In this day and age heroes are becoming harder to find. It seems that everybody is out for himself or herself and they don't think that they should have to live up to being a role model. Sports figures used to be great role models until they decided that they didn't have to be and could still make the big bucks. Sometimes it seems that in sports the worse you are as a role model the more you get paid. That's definitely got to change. We are very lucky to be involved in the sport of hockey where there are still players willing to be role models. One day that may change but for now we still have heroes like Gretzky, Lemieux, Sakic, and Kariya, to name a few.

When I was growing up we used to have heroes that we could pattern ourselves after. Whenever you had a tough decision to make you could say "what would 'my hero' do?" and it would make your decision making easier. Find yourself a role model. Do some research; remember what I told you about using the World Wide Web? Use it to find out as much as possible about the person you would like to be most like. If they are famous it will be easier to find information on them. Find out what they were like as a child, when they started playing hockey, what they are like now. Get into their lives and into their heads. Find their website if they have one and if possible write to them via e-mail. Get in contact with your "hero" and let them know that you consider them one.

A few heroes can be found if you are willing to look. A good starting point could be your own family. How much do you actually know about your own parents? Have you asked them the same questions that you would ask someone that the world would consider "famous"? What were they like as a kid? How did they become interested in doing what they do now? What is the most important thing in their life? What 'words of wisdom' would they give someone like you? Do you know what your mom or dad does for a living? Not where they work but what they do?

There is nothing sadder than someone who can tell you all about their favorite sports figure but can't tell you anything about their parents. After all, your parents are your biggest fans. Wouldn't it be nice to know a little bit more about them?

As a Personal Life Coach I ask people everyday about what they would change in their lives if they could. The amazing thing is that very few of them want to change the things that they did. Most of them want to change the things that they didn't do. The regrets they feel because they didn't take a chance or they didn't take advantage of someone else's wisdom or they just did nothing and let opportunity pass them by. Life isn't about accomplishing great things and becoming famous, although that is part of life. Life is really about remembering who we are destined to be; the greatness that is in each of us. No matter who you are right now you can change your life if you want.

It's all about the choices you make. Not other people's choices for you; your choices. You will have people along the way that will guide you because their intentions for you are of the highest. Along the way you will also encounter those people who really don't want you to reach your goals and destiny. You would find that your decisions would be much easier if you could look through everything and could see the end result of your actions. You can do this if you practice in your life like you should do in hockey. Think about this.

In hockey you don't always have the time to think about what to do. That's why you must allow yourself the time to make a choice. Did that make sense? No? Here's what I mean. The time to make a decision on how you will act or react to something is before you are faced with making the decision.

In sports many athletes are now doing what is known as visualization exercises. These are mental exercises that you put yourself through that enable you to make physical, mental and emotional choices more quickly during a game. It is said that your brain doesn't know the difference between reality and fantasy. If that is the case, you thinking about how you will react in a game designs a pattern within your brain that allows you to react spontaneously.

Outside of sports you can do the same type of thing with something called 'Absolutes'. Absolutes are things that you put into your life that will not change no matter what. An absolute might be that you will never take illegal drugs. How does that help you? Well, when you are offered an illegal drug by one of your friends you already no what your decision will be. That's a no brainer. The challenge is for you to set down a list of absolutes. Take the time to do this so that when you are faced with making a choice you respond in a way that will allow you to reach your goals in life.

Hockey is such a fast paced game, just like life, in order to play the game successfully you have to be able to create time and space for yourself. That means you have to anticipate where things are going and you have to put yourself in the position to make yourself available for a pass or in life terms, an opportunity.

So that's it. The beginning of your 'Life Lessons on Ice'. As you continue to play the wonderful game of ice hockey you will learn more about life. If you are smart you will put those lessons to good use. Here is your final Off-Ice Training Exercise. Start thinking about what you want your life to look like when you are finished. Imagine yourself writing your autobiography. What will you be putting into it? Will people want to read about your life? The exciting things you did. The people you knew. Will you have anything to write?

Now is the time. Right now…to start working on your own life story. Start planning. Start taking the steps towards a great life. Write it down and save it in a safe place. Someday you will find this piece of paper about your "vision" for your life and read what you wanted your life to be like. Maybe you will realize that it is your life! What a great feeling!

Good luck and remember, keep your head up and your stick on the ice!

Kim Tinkham is a freelance writer and a Licensed "Path" facilitator leading seminars to help kids and adults discover their mission statements for their lives. She is also a Personal Life Coach and Motivator and is one of the founders of UnitedHockeyMoms.

Kim lives with her husband Scott and son Garrett on a small ranch outside of Paradise, …Texas that is.

Kim can be reached via e-mail at
hockeymom@LifeLessonsOnIce.com
www.LifeLessonsOnIce.com

0-595-21685-4